The Best Book of
Dinosaurs

Chris Maynard

KINGFISHER

BOSTON

KINGFISHER

Kingfisher Publications Plc
New Penderel House
283–288 High Holborn
London WC1V 7HZ
www.kingfisherpub.com

First published by Kingfisher Publications Plc 1998
First published in this format 2005

10 9 8 7 6 5 4 3 2 1

1TR/0804/SHEN/PICA(PICA)/126.6MA

A CIP catalogue record for this book
is available from the British Library.

ISBN 0 7534 1094 X

Printed in Taiwan

Author: Christopher Maynard
Consultant: Professor Michael Benton
Editor: Vicky Weber
Illustrators: James Field, Chris Forsey,
 Christian Hook, Steve Kirk
Art Editor: Christina Fraser
Cover Designer: Mike Buckley
Production Controller: Eliot Sedman

Contents

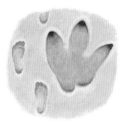

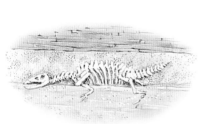

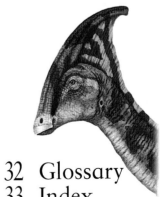

Dinosaur babies

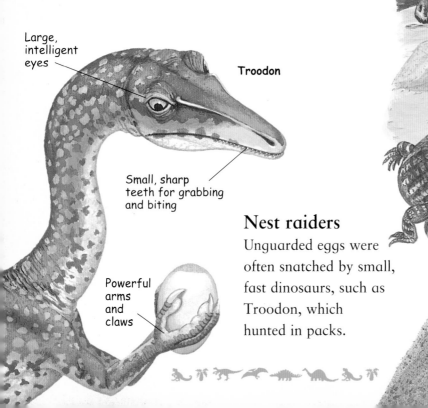

This Maiasaura mother dinosaur has been guarding her eggs for many weeks.
Now, one by one, her babies crack through their shells and wriggle out into the huge nest. Some stop to nibble at the blanket of rotting plants that has been keeping them warm. Others peer over the lip of the nest to take their first look at the world, 75 million years ago.

Large, intelligent eyes

Troodon

Small, sharp teeth for grabbing and biting

Powerful arms and claws

Nest raiders

Unguarded eggs were often snatched by small, fast dinosaurs, such as Troodon, which hunted in packs.

Dinosaur eggs

Dinosaurs were reptiles and they all laid eggs, like reptiles do today. Some eggs were round, but most were long and fat. The biggest were the size of a marrow.

Hen egg
8cm long

Maiasaura egg
12cm long

Protoceratops egg
20cm long

Hypselosaurus egg
30cm long

Bringing up baby

◀ Most dinosaurs laid their eggs in nests. A few, like Maiasaura, built their nests together, in a group or colony. Every year, they went back to the same place to lay their eggs.

▶ First, a Maiasaura mother dug a large, round hole. It was about the size of a garden paddling pool but much deeper.

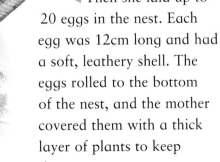

◀ Then she laid up to 20 eggs in the nest. Each egg was 12cm long and had a soft, leathery shell. The eggs rolled to the bottom of the nest, and the mother covered them with a thick layer of plants to keep them warm.

4 ▷ Day after day, the mother guarded her nest while the layer of plants rotted and kept the eggs warm.

5 ▷ The mother had to stay alert all the time to scare away nest robbers.

7 ▲ A young Maiasaura grew fast. It more than doubled in size by its first birthday. It had to be strong enough to keep up with the herd if it was going to survive.

8 ▷ The young dinosaurs stayed with the herd for the rest of their lives. Safety in numbers was their best defence against meat-eating dinosaurs that might attack and eat them.

6 ▲ Many weeks later, the eggs stirred, and cracked, and the first babies hatched. Within a few minutes they were able to walk about and forage for food.

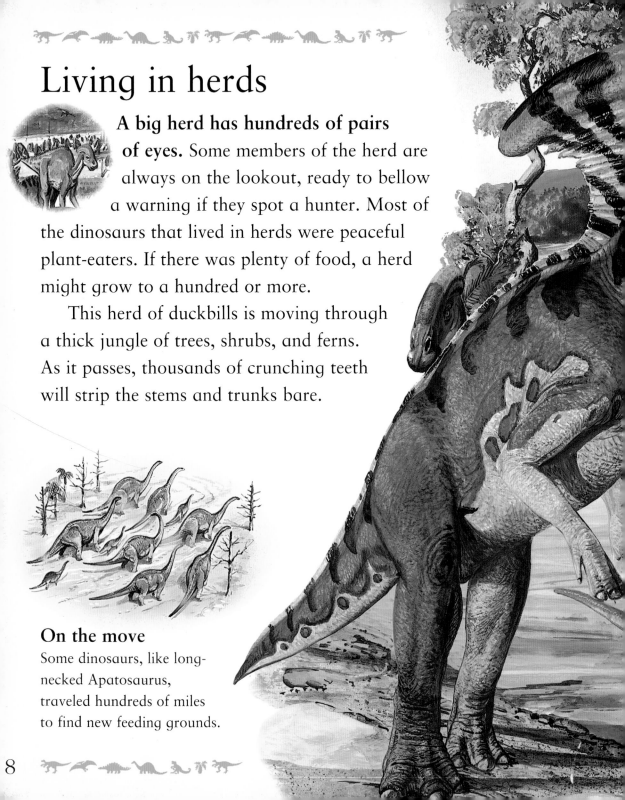

Living in herds

A big herd has hundreds of pairs of eyes. Some members of the herd are always on the lookout, ready to bellow a warning if they spot a hunter. Most of the dinosaurs that lived in herds were peaceful plant-eaters. If there was plenty of food, a herd might grow to a hundred or more.

This herd of duckbills is moving through a thick jungle of trees, shrubs, and ferns. As it passes, thousands of crunching teeth will strip the stems and trunks bare.

On the move
Some dinosaurs, like long-necked Apatosaurus, traveled hundreds of miles to find new feeding grounds.

Nose flap could be blown up like a balloon to honk

Edmontosaurus

Hollow horn

Tsintaosaurus

Bony axe-shaped crest

Lambeosaurus

Duckbilled dinosaurs

Duckbills had long flat snouts, a bit like a duck's bill. The scientific name for them is hadrosaurs. Most duckbills had bumps, horns or crests on their heads, and males usually had larger horns or crests than females. They were used to hoot or honk to the rest of the herd. In this way, a duckbill could signal all was well, or warn the herd of danger.

Guarding their young

When a herd of dinosaurs was on the move, like these Iguanodons, babies walked in the middle, guarded by their parents.

Pachycephalosaurus

Making a circle

A Triceratops herd backed into a circle if attacked, with babies in the centre and big males pointing their horns outwards.

Keeping watch

At night, dinosaurs settled down to sleep. In a large herd, some were always awake and moving about, like sentries on guard duty.

Fighting one another

In some big herds, males fought one another for a female or to sort out who was head of the herd, just like deer do today.

A Pachycephalosaurus had a thick dome-shaped skull to protect its brain during head-on fights. The males crashed into each other until the weaker one ran away.

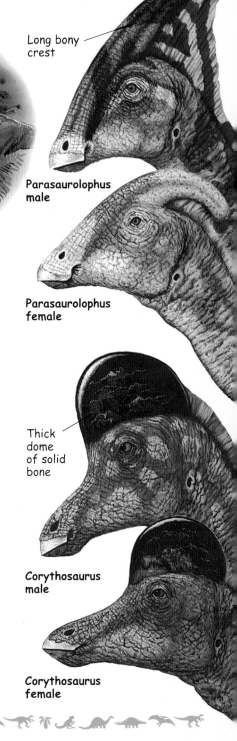

Long bony crest

Parasaurolophus male

Parasaurolophus female

Thick dome of solid bone

Corythosaurus male

Corythosaurus female

A gentle plant-eater

A giant head swings up, and the tall trees around it sway like grass. It strips a mouthful of juicy leaves and twigs with its stumpy, peg-shaped teeth. Then it swallows everything, without chewing, down a neck as long as a telephone pole.

This is Barosaurus—a giant plant-eater belonging to a group of long-necked dinosaurs called sauropods. Barosaurus was as tall as a five-story house. It needed to eat all day to fuel its huge body. But being huge made Barosaurus safe. Few hunters would dare attack anything so big.

Stomach stones

Big dinosaurs gulped down stones as they ate. The stones stayed in the gut, helping the stomach muscles grind leaves and twigs into a soft, sticky stew of plants. The dinosaur could digest this stew more easily.

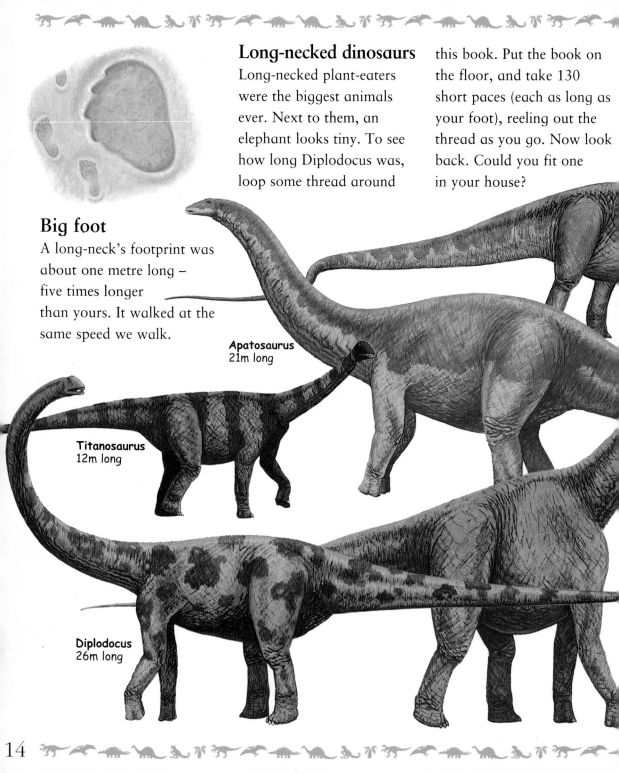

Long-necked dinosaurs

Long-necked plant-eaters were the biggest animals ever. Next to them, an elephant looks tiny. To see how long Diplodocus was, loop some thread around this book. Put the book on the floor, and take 130 short paces (each as long as your foot), reeling out the thread as you go. Now look back. Could you fit one in your house?

Big foot

A long-neck's footprint was about one metre long – five times longer than yours. It walked at the same speed we walk.

Apatosaurus
21m long

Titanosaurus
12m long

Diplodocus
26m long

Dinosaur diets

Dinosaurs lived on Earth for nearly 160 million years. During that time, the climate changed. That meant plants changed, too, and so did the dinosaurs.

Long-necks fed on pine needles, and tender shoots and leaves.

Duckbills ate crunchy pine cones and rubbery leaves from flowering shrubs.

Horned dinosaurs could manage tough ferns and stringy horsetails.

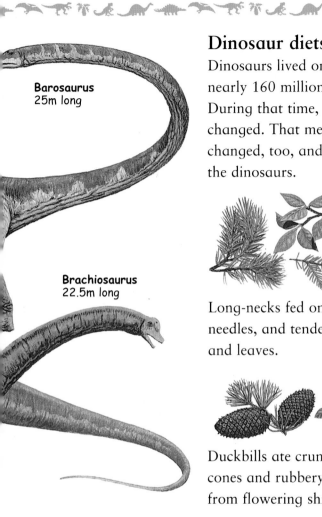

Barosaurus
25m long

Brachiosaurus
22.5m long

Elephant
4m long

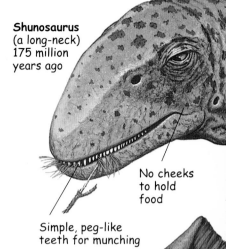

Shunosaurus (a long-neck) 175 million years ago

No cheeks to hold food

Simple, peg-like teeth for munching

Saurolophus (a duckbill) 80 million years ago

Hard, horny beak for chopping

Flat back teeth for grinding

Triceratops (a horned dinosaur) 70 million years ago

Sharp, narrow beak for slicing

Scissor-like teeth for cutting

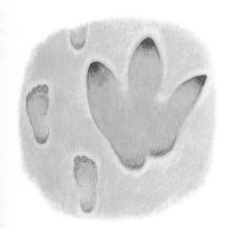

A fierce meat-eater

Lurking in the shadows of a redwood forest, the giant Tyrannosaurus sniffs the breeze and grunts. It can smell food nearby. Then it spies a mother Edmontosaurus and two youngsters at rest in a glade.

The big hunter stalks them quietly. Then, when it is just 380 feet away, it erupts from the trees like a roaring express train. In just a few seconds, well before its victims can rise and run away, it is on them. Its huge, heavy jaws tear into one of the young dinosaurs with a wild, killing bite.

Quick foot

This is Tyrannosaurus's footprint. It had three toes, with a giant talon on each toe, and it was 2 feet long—twice as long as a human footprint.

Tyrannosaurus could run as fast as a horse, at almost 24 miles per hour.

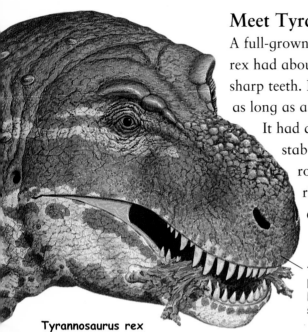

Meet Tyrannosaurus

A full-grown Tyrannosaurus rex had about 50 razor-sharp teeth. Each tooth was as long as a banana.

It had a sharp point to stab its victim, and rough edges to rip through skin and flesh.

Tyrannosaurus's head was 4 feet long—big enough to swallow you whole

Tyrannosaurus rex

When old teeth wore out, new ones grew in their place

Dilophosaurus

Allosaurus

Albertosaurus

Big meat-eaters

These three fierce hunters were all related to Tyrannosaurus and had sharp teeth and claws. None, though, were quite as big. A full-grown Tyrannosaurus was tall enough to look through a second-floor window.

Going hunting

▷ Allosaurus wakes up and rises slowly from the ground. It uses its small arms to balance as it rears up on its hind legs.

▽ A few hours later, its sharp eyes spot a herd of plant-eaters. Slowly it creeps up on them, looking for a likely victim. Allosaurus waits, and waits, for just the right moment.

◁ Its last meal was four days ago, and now it is very hungry. It finds an old carcass and tears at the bones, but there is little meat left to ease its hunger.

▲ A young dinosaur foolishly lags behind the herd. Allosaurus bursts from its hiding place in a short, swift sprint and grabs its victim by the neck. Its fangs sink deep and tear out a huge slab of flesh in one lethal bite.

▷ Allosaurus tears out chunk after chunk of flesh and bone and swallows them whole. It gorges till its belly is bloated. Then it staggers away to lie down and doze for hours, just like a well-fed lion.

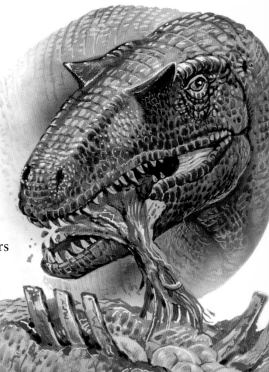

Pack attack!

Sauropelta is bigger than a bison and bristling with armor, but the pack of Deinonychus still attacks.
The wolf-sized hunters charge at Sauropelta from all sides, trying to rake its hide with their fangs and slash open its underbelly with their giant claws. But their prey's hide is so studded with spikes, horns, and bony knobs that they don't do much damage.

One attacker is knocked to the ground by Sauropelta's swinging tail and is trampled in the dust. The ferocious pack will soon give up and search for an easier meal.

Sickle-shaped claw

Deinonychus foot

Terrible claw
Deinonychus had a huge claw on the second toe of each back foot. The claw swiveled up as it ran and swung down like a slashing knife blade when it attacked.

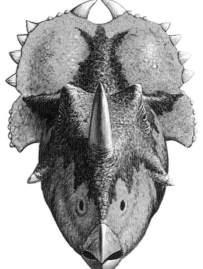

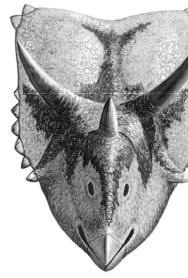

Triceratops

Centrosaurus

Chasmosaurus

Armored dinosaurs

Plant-eaters had many ways of protecting themselves. Some lived in herds and found safety in numbers. A few were just too big to be attacked. Others had body armor to defend themselves, and horns or spiked tails to fight with.

The three horned dinosaurs above had huge, bony neck frills. If an attacker tried to bite them, it would break its teeth.

Ankylosaurus was like a four-legged tank, with thick, leathery skin and bony lumps and spikes all over its head and back. If attacked, it crouched down to protect its underbelly.

Ankylosaurus

Heavy, clubbed tail

Bony spikes

Soft underbelly

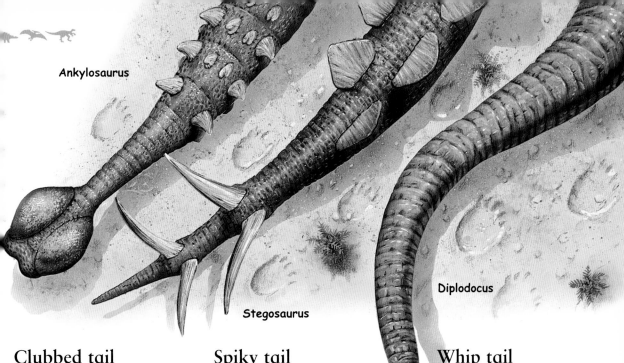

Ankylosaurus

Stegosaurus

Diplodocus

Clubbed tail

Ankylosaurus had a long tail that ended in a heavy bony club up to 4 feet wide. The dinosaur swung its tail at an attacker. One blow was powerful enough to shatter bone, or even kill.

Spiky tail

Stegosaurus had a thick tail that bristled with four large spikes. To defend itself, it turned its back on attackers and swung its tail back and forth to give a lethal blow.

Whip tail

Diplodocus had a long tail that was as thin and flexible as a whip. If attacked, it lashed it to and fro. Its weight could land a blow hard enough to knock an attacker off its feet.

Run for your life!

The sound of pounding hooves drums across an open plain as a herd of long-legged, ostrichlike dinosaurs runs for its life. Smaller dinosaurs like these didn't have horns or clubbed tails to protect them from meat-eaters. What they did have was speed. Struthiomimus was as fast as a racehorse and could outrun almost any attacker.

Freeze

Tiny Compsognathus used its speed to catch lizards or frogs. If hunted by a larger dinosaur, it hid and froze in the undergrowth.

Safety in numbers

Like other small plant-eaters, Lesothosaurus relied on the rest of its herd to spot danger, and on its speed to get away.

Raid and run

Oviraptor was fast enough to catch darting lizards or small mammals. It used speed and agility to escape from its enemies, too.

Run like the wind

Hypsilophodon was one of the fastest small plant-eaters. As it fled, it dodged from side to side to escape claws and jaws.

Then they were gone

After ruling the world for 160 million years, all the dinosaurs died out. Why? It's most likely that the dinosaurs became extinct after a meteorite smashed into Earth, exploding with the power of a thousand volcanoes. The explosion burned and killed everything for thousands of miles. It also flung up enough dust to block out the sun's light and heat. Earth became cold, and many creatures— including the dinosaurs—perished.

Avimimus—a fast, feathered dinosaur

Roadrunner— a relative of Avimimus?

Dinosaur survivors
Some scientists think that dinosaurs were the ancestors of modern birds.

⚠ A huge meteorite, 6 miles wide and traveling at 60,000 miles per hour, hit Earth in Central America.

⚠ It formed a crater almost 120 miles wide and threw a massive cloud of dust into the sky.

⚠ The dust blocked out the sunlight for many years. The air became cold. Many plants and animals died.

How fossils are made

⚠ Millions of years ago, a dinosaur dies. It is buried under soft sand or mud, perhaps after falling into a lake or river.

⚠ The skin and flesh soon rot away, but the hard bones do not rot. They slowly become fossils, and the sand and mud surrounding them turn into rock.

⚠ The rock containing the fossils is worn away by wind and rain, and the fossils appear at the surface.

Big buried bones

We only know about the dinosaurs that lived millions of years ago because of clues they left behind, such as fossils of their bones, teeth, and claws. When fossils of dinosaur bones are discovered, scientists called paleontologists clear away the rock that surrounds the fossils. They also measure and photograph them. Then they dig them out of the ground and wrap them in a cocoon of cloth soaked in plaster. This keeps them safe on their way to a museum.

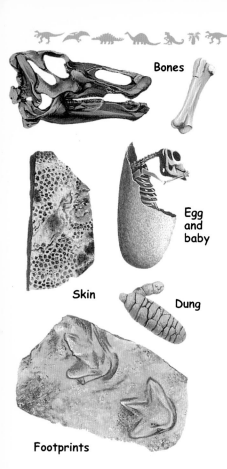

Bones

Egg
and
baby

Skin

Dung

Footprints

Bone puzzle

▶ When the fossils have been moved to a museum, they are broken out of their plaster cases with saws, hammers, and chisels.

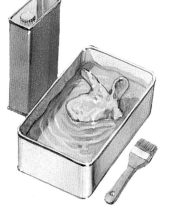

◀ If the fossil has been lying in a rock called limestone, it may be given a bath in weak vinegar to help wash away some of the limestone rock.

All kinds of fossils

Scientists do not only find fossils of bones. Far more often, they find fossils of footprints. Their size and how far apart they are tell us how big and how fast the dinosaur was. We also have fossils of dinosaur eggs, and sometimes, fossils that show scaly skin. We even have fossils of dinosaur dung!

▶ Dentist's drills, toothpicks, and magnifying glasses are used to clean the last traces of rock from each bone. A dinosaur has over 300 bones, so it can take months to do this delicate job.

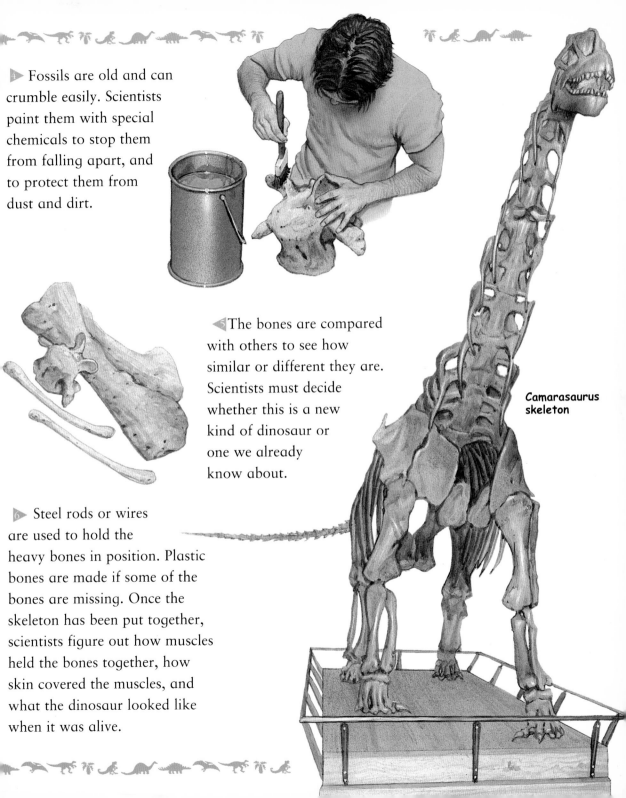

Fossils are old and can crumble easily. Scientists paint them with special chemicals to stop them from falling apart, and to protect them from dust and dirt.

The bones are compared with others to see how similar or different they are. Scientists must decide whether this is a new kind of dinosaur or one we already know about.

Steel rods or wires are used to hold the heavy bones in position. Plastic bones are made if some of the bones are missing. Once the skeleton has been put together, scientists figure out how muscles held the bones together, how skin covered the muscles, and what the dinosaur looked like when it was alive.

Camarasaurus skeleton

Glossary

armor A thick layer of bone just under the skin of some dinosaurs—large bone plates in some, smaller knobs of bone in others. This prevented hunters from biting through the skin.

climate The usual, year-round weather of a place. In jungles the climate is hot and wet, in deserts it is dry.

colony A group of animals that comes together to lay eggs and raise its young. A colony is harder for a hunter to attack than a single nest and mother.

Cretaceous The third and last great age of dinosaurs, which lasted from 145 to 65 million years ago. By the end of it, all the dinosaurs had died out.

dinosaurs Large land-living reptiles of the Triassic, Jurassic, or Cretaceous period. The name is from the Ancient Greek for "terrible lizard."

duckbills A group of plant-eating dinosaurs that had wide snouts like a duck's bill and moved on their two hind legs.

extinction The death of every last one of a group of plants or animals. The dinosaurs became extinct 65 million years ago.

fossil The remains of an ancient plant or animal. All we know about dinosaurs comes from their fossils.

herd A large group of animals. Many dinosaurs lived in herds for protection —a herd has many ears and eyes to detect an attacker.

Jurassic The second great age of dinosaurs, from 205 to 145 million years ago.

meat-eater An animal that eats the flesh of other animals, by killing them or by feeding on already dead bodies.

meteorite A chunk of rock that hurtles through space and crashes to Earth. Most are so small that we hardly notice them. The few big ones cause huge explosions.

paleontologist A scientist who studies ancient plants and animals—mainly from fossils that are millions of years old.

plant-eater An animal that feeds on plants, not on other animals. Most dinosaurs were plant-eaters. So are most animals today.

predator An animal that hunts other animals.

prey An animal that is being hunted by another animal.

reptile A cold-blooded, scaly, four-legged animal that lays its eggs on land. Dinosaurs were reptiles. So are lizards, snakes, crocodiles, and turtles.

sauropods The name for all large, long-necked, plant-eating dinosaurs, such as Diplodocus.

skeleton The framework of bones that holds up the body of any animal.

Triassic The first of the three great ages of dinosaurs, from 250 to 205 million years ago.